Not a
Drop
to Drink

Water for a Thirsty World

Not a Drop to Drink

Water for a Thirsty World

By Michael Burgan
Dr. Peter H. Gleick, Consultant

NATIONAL
GEOGRAPHIC
Washington, D.C.

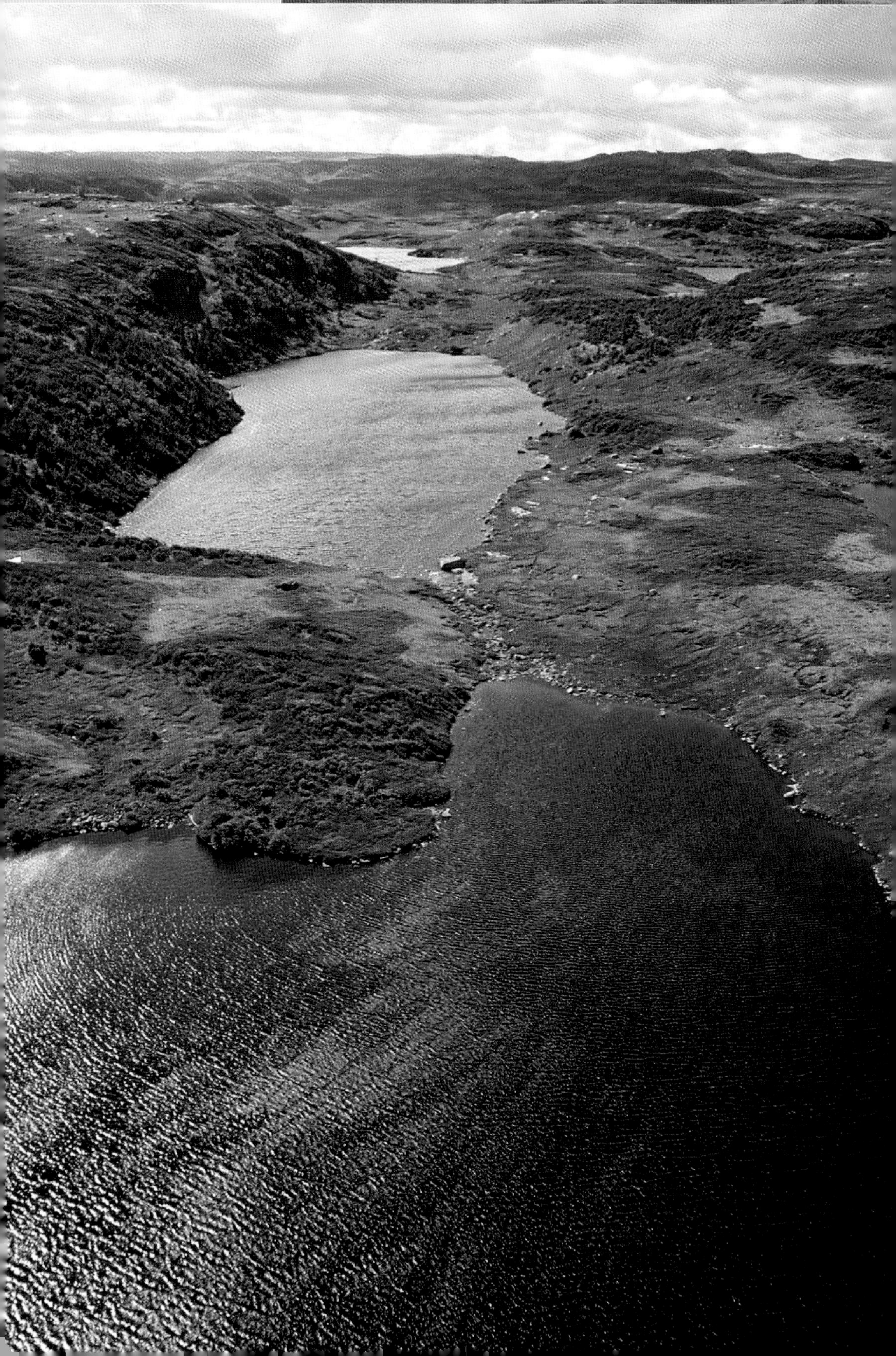

Contents

< Mountains surrounding bodies of water in Newfoundland, Canada, are experiencing snow melt earlier in the season than ever before. As global warming increases, glaciers around the globe are receding, putting the water supply for the world's population in jeopardy.

< A remotely operated vehicle (ROV) is fitted with a rock cutter so scientists can draw samples of
water from beneath the ocean floor.

From the Consultant

We are creatures of water. We evolved from the oceans, and if we didn't now live on the dry land, we would call the planet "Water," not "Earth," because it is largely covered with this most precious resource. We depend on water for all we do, from growing the food we eat to cleaning our homes and clothes to producing the goods and services we consume every day. Yet the world is in a water crisis. Billions of people still lack safe drinking water and adequate sanitation, leading to unnecessary illness and death. Aquatic ecosystems are suffering because humans consume or contaminate water that they too need to survive. Countries and regions fight over access to increasingly scarce water resources. Our oceans are overfished, underprotected, and still largely mysterious to us. And we are changing the very climate of the planet. The good news is that smart people around the world are studying our water resources, learning

how those resources can be used carefully, and helping all of us move from a world in crisis to a world that supports people, birds, fish, animals, and the natural environment sustainably into the future. Read and learn what others, and you, can do to protect our precious water.

Dr. Peter H. Gleick

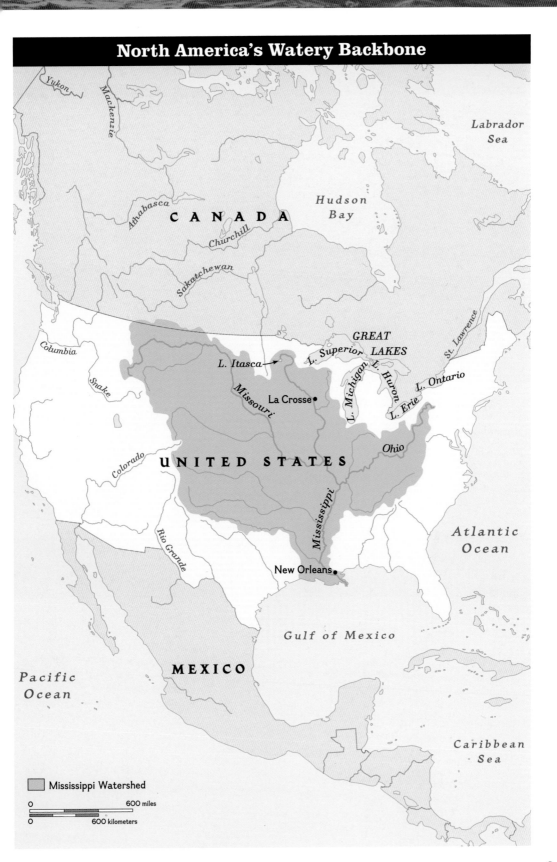

North America's Watery Backbone

Yukon

Mackenzie

Athabasca

Churchill

Sakatchewan

CANADA

Hudson
Bay

Labrador
Sea

Columbia

Snake

GREAT LAKES

L. Itasca

L. Superior

L. Michigan

L. Huron

L. Erie

L. Ontario

St. Lawrence

Missouri

La Crosse

UNITED STATES

Colorado

Ohio

Mississippi

Rio Grande

New Orleans

Atlantic
Ocean

MEXICO

Gulf of Mexico

Pacific
Ocean

Caribbean
Sea

Mississippi Watershed

0   600 miles

0   600 kilometers

∧ **1920s · Southern California** was the scene of water shortages and conflict as early as 1920.

> **1977 · Mid-ocean vents,** cracks in the ocean floor that shoot out streams of hot water full of minerals and bacteria, were first discovered by geologists in 1977, in the Galapagos Rift off the coast of South America.

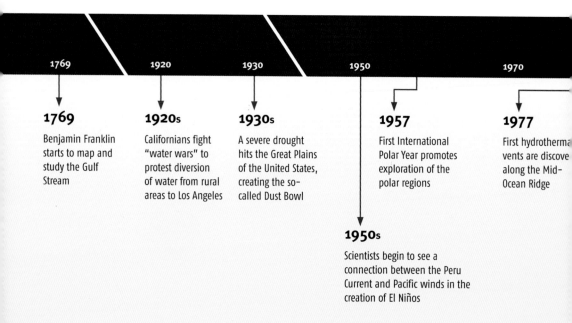

1769	1920	1930	1950	1970

1769

Benjamin Franklin starts to map and study the Gulf Stream

1920s

Californians fight "water wars" to protest diversion of water from rural areas to Los Angeles

1930s

A severe drought hits the Great Plains of the United States, creating the so-called Dust Bowl

1957

First International Polar Year promotes exploration of the polar regions

1977

First hydrotherma vents are discove along the Mid-Ocean Ridge

1950s

Scientists begin to see a connection between the Peru Current and Pacific winds in the creation of El Niños

> **1997** · Lower water levels in Lake Superior reveal land mass.

∧ **1980s** · Dr. Nancy Rabalais logs data from an over-the-side oxygen meter in the Gulf of Mexico Dead Zone.

> **2007** · A once-submerged tree is revealed as water levels drop at Lake Lanier in Gainesville, Georgia, endangering the water supply for more than 3 million residents in the Atlanta region.

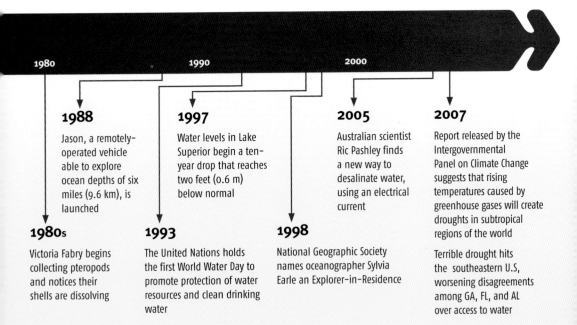

1980   1990   2000

1988
Jason, a remotely-operated vehicle able to explore ocean depths of six miles (9.6 km), is launched

1980s
Victoria Fabry begins collecting pteropods and notices their shells are dissolving

1997
Water levels in Lake Superior begin a ten-year drop that reaches two feet (0.6 m) below normal

1993
The United Nations holds the first World Water Day to promote protection of water resources and clean drinking water

2005
Australian scientist Ric Pashley finds a new way to desalinate water, using an electrical current

1998
National Geographic Society names oceanographer Sylvia Earle an Explorer-in-Residence

2007
Report released by the Intergovernmental Panel on Climate Change suggests that rising temperatures caused by greenhouse gases will create droughts in subtropical regions of the world

Terrible drought hits the southeastern U.S, worsening disagreements among GA, FL, and AL over access to water

Water Everywhere

CHAPTER 1

Seeking Cold, Hard Facts

At the southern tip of the world, international teams of scientists on the Western Antarctic Peninsula measure water and air temperatures. High above Earth, satellites collect images of the region, pinpointing the location of glaciers. Through the Internet, the researchers share data with each other and scientists back at home. Taken together, the information collected helps scientists learn how climate change, sometimes called global warming, affects the world's most remote continent.

This work is part of a project called ClicOPEN, for **Cli**mate **Co**astal **Pen**insula, and it is one of many scientific events underway during the

◁ Glaciers throughout the Antarctic Peninsula are receding, affecting ocean water all over the world.

International Polar Year (IPY). This IPY (2007–2009), the fourth in history, is an ongoing international effort to better understand the life, climate, water, and ice that define Earth's two polar regions.

In recent years, global warming has become a major concern for the polar regions—and the rest of the planet, too. Over the last 50 years, the air temperature in parts of Antarctica has risen about 4.5°F (2.5°C)—more than any other known increase in the past 500 years. The Antarctic is still a frozen land—

temperatures in some areas average –8°F (–22°C). But the recent rise in temperatures has melted some of the continent's glaciers. One chunk that melted in the past few years was the size of California!

Looking for Answers

Doris Abele, a scientist at the Alfred Wegener Institute for Polar and Marine Science, leads the ClicOPEN team. She expressed the mission's main goal: "We will learn how air warming affects glaciers and what physical changes it brings for land

∧ At the Dallmann Laboratory in Jubany, Antarctica, research is conducted on how climate change affects Antarctic habitats.

∧ Field scientists in diving gear off the coast of Potter Cove, King George Island, Antarctica, prepare to take samples from beneath the ocean's surface.

and ocean surfaces at the Antarctic Peninsula." The ClicOPEN scientists represent 16 nations, including the United States, Canada, Spain, and Russia. They operate out of four existing research stations on Antarctica, plus a new one built at the southern end of Argentina. A Polish fishing boat has been turned into a floating research platform, and is being used to map the sea bottom along the coast. The ClicOPEN scientists also use a remotely operated vehicle to explore the waters.

The results from ClicOPEN should help scientists predict what will happen as temperatures continue to rise and more ice melts. Dr. Abele thinks the IPY plays a key role in raising public knowledge about the importance of the polar regions:

"It is important to realize...what it means for the earth systems when ice shields and glaciers collapse at the remote ends of the world."

∧ A diver under the sea ice in Antarctica

Big Help from Tiny Tubes

Far from Earth's coldest continent, in sunny California, research done in a lab could help bring water to billions of thirsty people. Scientists Olgica Bakajin and Aleksandr Noy lead a research team at the Lawrence Livermore National Laboratory in northern California. Peering through powerful microscopes, they study nanotubes—tubes made of carbon that are 50,000 times narrower than human hair. Bakajin and Noy have found a way to create a membrane out of billions of the tubes. Water molecules can pass through the tiny tubes, but molecules of solids cannot.

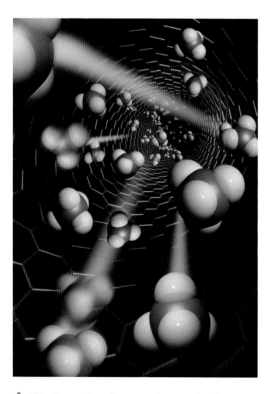

∧ This illustration shows methane molecules flowing through a carbon nanotube. Only water molecules can pass through the holes in the membrane.

The nanotube membrane could be a big help in desalination—the removal of salt and other solids from seawater, so it can be used for drinking water. Current methods are expensive, as they require large amounts of energy to push water through existing membranes. If the nanotube system can be perfected, water could be purified faster and cheaper than it can be now. That would be a big plus for the one billion people around the world who do not have access to clean drinking water. Another two billion people face water shortages, and that number is expected to grow in the years to come.

Why Water Matters

Water is an essential resource for life on Earth. Plants and animals, including humans, need water in order to survive. The adult human body is about 55 percent water, and a person can live only about eight days without drinking water. (By comparison, a person can live for several weeks without food.)

Altogether, water in all its forms covers more than 70 percent of Earth's surface. The abundance of water, however, does not mean that humans and other life forms always have all the water they need. Only about 3 percent of the world's water is fresh water; the rest contains salt and is not drinkable. More than two-thirds of the fresh water is unavailable for drinking. It sits frozen solid as glaciers and ice caps in the world's coldest climates. Another 30 percent of the fresh water is underground, making it hard to tap for drinking. Rivers and lakes provide most of the water drunk on Earth.

But water provides much more than a refreshing drink on a hot day. It also provides habitat for freshwater and saltwater fish that people eat. Waterways provide transportation routes for vessels of all sizes. Surface water in the form of lakes and rivers provides recreation for boaters and swimmers. Water is a source of energy too—a rushing river or the movement of ocean tides can be harnessed to spin giant turbines used to create electricity. And a process called ocean thermal energy

∧ Water is one of the world's most precious commodities, sustaining the life of our planet and its people.

conversion taps into the power stored in surface water after it is heated by the sun. All these uses of water also provide jobs for millions of people.

∨ The waters of the Colorado River were dammed to create power at the Hoover Dam.

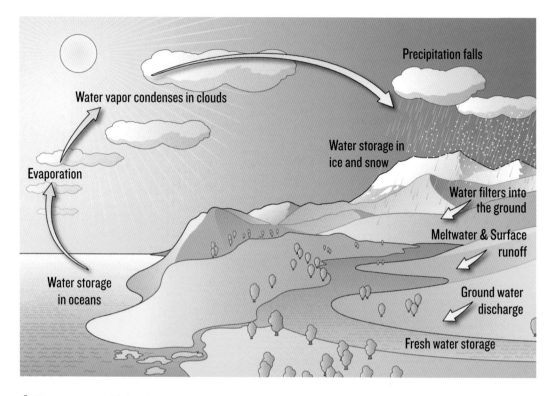

Λ The water you drink today may once have been rainwater that ran off a dinosaur's back.

The Water Cycle

Water is a finite resource that moves all around us in an endless cycle. Fueling this movement of water is the sun. Its energy heats the oceans and other large bodies of water, turning some of the water into vapor. This vapor, along with some water that evaporates from the ground or is released by plants, is carried by air currents into the atmosphere. Cool air high above the ground changes the vapor into tiny water droplets, which form around even smaller bits of dust, smoke, or salt in the air. These droplets then combine to form clouds. When some of the droplets are large enough,

they fall as rain, snow, or other precipitation. A single raindrop has a volume that is a million times that of a cloud droplet.

Some precipitation takes the form of ice, which over time slowly melts, sending water into rivers, streams, and oceans. Rain also falls into these bodies of water or flows into them after traveling along Earth's surface. Other rainwater goes into the ground, where it moves very slowly or is stored. Over time, some of this groundwater also enters rivers, streams, lakes, and oceans, where the sun's heat continues to drive the cycle all over again.

Studying Water

Although scientists know the basic pattern of the water cycle, they are still learning what factors may be changing the way the cycle works. They record climate conditions related to the water cycle, such as cloud cover and precipitation. They hope to learn whether changes are part of a natural pattern or are somehow influenced by human actions.

Global warming results when people's activities release certain gases into Earth's atmosphere. That human-made warming has far-reaching effects on climate and water. Researchers want to understand how those effects in certain areas, such as the Antarctic, might threaten plants and animals. Other human activities, such as polluting water sources with harmful chemicals or using up groundwater, limit the availability of drinking water in some areas.

Water research can do more than just detect or solve a problem. Dr. Abele of ClicOPEN sees her project and other IPY efforts stirring the curiosity of students, so one day they might pursue science as a career. Some scientists want to know more about the life forms that inhabit water, especially along deep ocean floors. Resources underwater could also possibly be mined for use on land or turned into new medicines.

In the chapters to come, you will learn more about the scientists who

Accidental Science

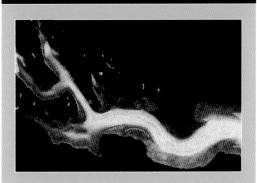

Λ **When exposed to a radio-frequency field, salt water appears to burst into flame.**

Part of the thrill of science is coming upon the unexpected. Researchers never know exactly where their work will lead. John Kanzius, a Florida engineer, was hoping to find a way to use radio waves to treat cancer. Instead, he made the startling discovery that the radio waves created a spark in a tube of salt water. Then he saw that the water could burn as long as the radio waves were zipping through it. In 2007, Rustum Roy of Pennsylvania State University confirmed Kanzius's work. The radio waves separate the salt, oxygen, and hydrogen in the salt water. The process could offer another way to desalinate ocean water if the technology can be made commercially available at a reasonable cost.

are working in many ways to preserve the world's most precious resource. You will also learn about cutting-edge technology designed to help people in remote regions of the world, and large-scale projects that may provide energy for entire countries. The future of the planet depends, in part, on these people and the projects to which they devote themselves.

Warming Water

CHAPTER 2

A Problem With Shells

About twenty years ago, California biologist Victoria Fabry was doing research on microscopic sea life in the waters off Alaska. She collected some samples of pteropods in a jar of water. Pteropods are tiny sea snails, also called plankton. As the pteropods sat in the seawater, Fabry saw their shells starting to dissolve. Intrigued by this oddity, she decided to keep the samples she had collected.

As the years passed, Fabry read reports by other scientists suggesting that rising levels of the gas carbon dioxide (CO_2) were affecting the ability of some plankton to create the calcium carbonate shells that usually cover them.

< Ice flows in the Arctic region are breaking up earlier each spring as a result of warmer water temperatures, affecting plants and animals such as the pteropods collected in the Gulf of Alaska (pictured here) by Dr. Victoria Fabry.

Fabry then did further testing with the pteropods she had collected and confirmed that higher levels of CO_2 in the water damaged their shells.

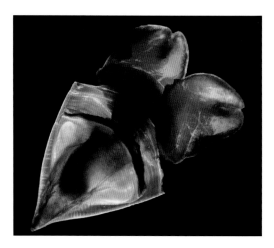

∧ A pteropod like the ones studied by Dr. Fabry

Greenhouse Gases and the Oceans

Carbon dioxide is one of several gases sometimes called greenhouse gases. These gases collect in the atmosphere above Earth and prevent heat from escaping. Some of the gases occur naturally. Methane, for example, is released by rotting organic matter in wetlands. (This is what makes swamps smelly.) CO_2 is part of the breath humans and other living creatures exhale. But in the past two hundred years, human activity has increased the amount of greenhouse gases released into the atmosphere. The use of fertilizers in

∨ Dr. Victoria Fabry collecting samples of pteropods for study. Dr. Fabry's observations, taken over two decades, have led to theories of how global warming affects ocean life.

farming and the burning of coal and petroleum (fossil fuels) for energy are two main causes of this increase.

Not all the extra CO2 released, however, goes into the atmosphere. A report that Fabry co-wrote noted that in the past 25 years, about 20 percent of human-created CO2 was absorbed by the world's forests, while the oceans took in even more—30 percent. Each day, the oceans take in more than 20 million tons of carbon dioxide produced by humans. But absorbing that CO2 is taking a toll on the oceans. CO2 readily dissolves in water, forming carbonic acid, which raises the acidity of the water. And it is those rising acid levels that damage the shells of pteropods and other plankton.

Dr. Christopher Sabine has spent many days at sea, from Antarctica to Alaska, collecting water samples. Sabine works for the National Oceanic and Atmospheric Administration (NOAA). The samples he and other scientists collect show tiny but clear increases in acid levels. Using data that project how much CO2 the oceans will continue to absorb, scientists predict that increased acid levels will have a noticeable impact.

∧ Dr. Christopher Sabine installs a carbon sensor on a mooring off the coast of Washington state.

Oceans in Motion

The oceans also play an important role in regulating the weather, thanks to their currents. The ocean currents take energy from the sun and transport oxygen, energy, and nutrients to all parts of the world.

The constantly moving currents are sometimes called a global conveyor belt. In the North Atlantic Ocean, cold water on the surface sinks and is replaced by warm, salty water that has moved northward from the Equator. As the warm water releases heat to the atmosphere, it becomes colder and starts to sink. Meanwhile, the cold water originating in the North Atlantic travels to the

Indian and Pacific Oceans, where it is heated. The surface water, made saltier by evaporation, absorbs the energy of the sun's rays. This water then begins to move northward again. The entire process is sometimes called ocean overturning. One complete cycle of the water from cold to warm to cold again takes a thousand years.

Clues From the Past

Paleoceanographers are looking to the past to try to understand the present—and future—state of ocean currents and temperatures. Karen Bice of the Woods Hole Oceanographic Institution is a paleoclimatologist, a scientist who studies ancient (paleo) climates. She and a research team sailed on a special ship equipped with a large drill to explore the seafloor off the South American nation of Suriname, not far from the Equator. The drill retrieved samples of fossils that have sat on the ocean floor for millions of years. The deeper the samples, the longer ago they settled on the floor. Bice and the other scientists then studied fossilized shells from the different depths. Changes in the shells over time indicated changing temperatures in

Scientists from the National Oceanic and Atmospheric Administration collect water samples in the Pacific Ocean. NOAA monitors the conditions of the oceans and atmosphere around the globe.

the ocean. Their conclusion: Millions of years ago, the water in this part of the Atlantic Ocean reached temperatures between 91° and 107°F (33° and 43°C). (Current temperatures for the Atlantic are approximately 25°F (14°C) below this.)

Bice and the other scientists concluded that current CO_2 levels in the water may lead to even greater temperatures than predicted. Bice said that higher temperatures in the tropics could affect weather patterns in other parts of the world.

∧ Paleoclimatologist Karen Bice studies data collected from sediment on the ocean floor.

Studying Decay

Other paleoceanographers study ancient dirt, rocks, and other materials that settled to the bottom of a body of water. The scientists also examine different varieties, or isotopes, of the element uranium that are found on the ocean floor. These isotopes decay at different rates. Measuring the amount of the various isotopes in the sediment tells the scientists how quickly ocean overturning occurred in the past. Work by Woods Hole geologist Delia Oppo, among others, suggests that fresh water added to the oceans by the melting of glaciers slows down the ocean overturning, sending less heat and warm water northward.

In recent years, glaciers and ice packs at the poles and in mountain regions have been melting rapidly. The U.S. National Ice Center studies ice around the globe. Its scientists use ground observations and satellites to measure the extent of ice and its retreat. In the Arctic, sea ice levels reached record lows in 2007. This and other melt-offs around the globe have put more fresh water into the salty oceans.

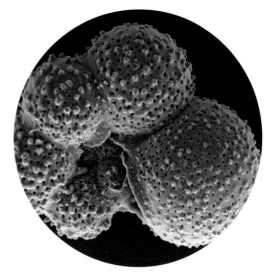

> A skeleton of 90-million-year-old plankton collected off the coast of Suriname, in the tropical Atlantic ocean

If global warming leads to more fresh water in the oceans, it could actually mean a cooling off for some parts of the world. Currently, the ocean current called the Gulf Stream carries warm water and air across the Atlantic Ocean to parts of northern Europe. A slowdown in ocean overturning would weaken the

"Current Events"

Benjamin Franklin was always interested in exploring the world around him. Although best known as a witty writer and a diplomat for the young United States, Franklin was also one of the great scientists of the 18th century. He learned from a sea captain about a current that seemed to push ships along as they sailed eastward from New England to London. Franklin had the captain mark the current's location on a map, which Franklin then published for other sailors to use. In the years that followed, Franklin was the first scientist to study the current, which was already called the Gulf Stream. He took the temperature of samples of ocean water to determine the exact location of the current, since it was already known that the current was warmer than the water on either side of it. He also measured wind

∧ Benjamin Franklin conducted early studies of the ocean current known as the Gulf Stream.

and current speeds along the Gulf Stream. Franklin then promoted the idea that his captain friend already knew. Ships could travel faster going east across the Atlantic if they rode in the current, which moved faster than the surrounding waters. Likewise, avoiding the current on the way west made for a quicker trip.

< The first image shows Arctic sea ice concentration in 1979. The second image shows sea ice concentration in 2003.

Gulf Stream, bringing cooler air to Great Britain, France, and other nations. Scientists have already noted that the circulation of the Gulf Stream is weaker than it was several decades ago. But even if temperatures fall because of a weakened Gulf Stream, rising temperatures from global warming will balance out Europe's temperatures.

More Quakes?

The melting of glaciers and an increase of fresh water in the oceans could also cause more earthquakes and volcanic eruptions. NASA scientists believe the melting of glaciers decreases the weight above rocky plates just below Earth's surface. The grinding of these tectonic plates causes earthquakes. With less weight above them, the plates can move more freely, increasing the risk of an earthquake. As far as volcanoes, Bill McGuire, of England's Benfield UCL (University College London) Hazard Research Centre, says the added weight of new water in the oceans from melting glaciers could cause bends in Earth's crust along the plates. That bending could be enough to start a volcanic eruption.

V Smoke rises from the Barren Island volcano, 135 kilometers (84 miles) east of Port Blair, India, on March 25, 2007.

Disappearing Water

CHAPTER 3

The Heat Is On

Almost 2.5 miles (4 km) above sea level, D. P. Dobhal braves the cold air and threat of avalanches to carry out his work. Dobhal, a geologist, studies glaciers in the Himalayas of Central Asia. The mountains are the world's tallest, which may be why the glaciers that top their peaks are among the least studied in the world.

Dobhal's most recent effort is studying the slow melt of a glacier called Chorabari. Its melting waters form the Mandakini River, which eventually flows into India's mighty Ganges River. Along the way, the glacier-fed Mandakini provides water for drinking and irrigation.

< The Chorabari glacier in the Himalayan Mountains sweeps down from the Kedarnath mountain peak. It has retreated an average of around 30 feet per year for the past three years.

> Dr. D. P. Dobhal (right) atop a glacier covered by dirt in the Himalayas. The team measures the mass of the ice in this spot.

At different times during the year, Dobhal and his assistants drill 13-foot (4-m) holes into the glacier. They then place bamboo poles in the holes. The poles serve as yardsticks to measure the mass of the ice. After several years of making this mountain trek and measuring Chorabari, Dobhal has reached a clear conclusion: The glacier is melting rapidly. Its snout, the spot where the melting water rushes out to the surface, has moved about 30 feet (9 m) up the mountain each of the last several years.

In the Andes of Peru, Lonnie Thompson of Ohio State University has tracked glaciers for 30 years. In his work, Thompson drills deep into the ice to remove samples. The different isotopes of oxygen stored in the ice record change in temperature over time. The samples, Thompson says, show a clear trend of rising temperatures in the Peruvian Andes over the last 50 years. The warming temperatures have sped up the melting of the glaciers. Peru's Quelccaya, the world's largest tropical ice cap, is retreating ten times faster than it did during the 1960s. According to Thompson, "things are dramatically changing."

< Scientists drill into the ice on Huascaran, a mountain in the West Andes range of Peru.

Normally, precipitation adds to the glacier by turning to ice. But now, even extra precipitation in the Andes is not enough for the glaciers to replenish themselves from year to year. As in the Himalayas, the shrinking of the glaciers could mean water shortages in the long run for the people who live along the rivers fed by glacial melt.

Short Supplies

The melting of mountain glaciers highlights the crucial importance of water on Earth. Life on Earth is bordered by water, in the oceans and the ice caps. But as noted in Chapter 1, just a tiny fraction of that water is available for drinking or irrigation. Across the world, millions of people have trouble getting water for their

daily needs. And even small changes in climate or human activity can affect how much water is available in different parts of the world.

Part of the problem comes from nature: Droughts, extended periods without rain, can occur in climates of all kinds. Another problem is that water might be right under a person's feet, but too hard to reach. Some precipitation enters the ground through rock and soil. Underground, the water can collect into areas called aquifers. Using drills, humans can tap into the aquifers for their water needs. Water is drawn up from the

▼ In 2002, mountain climbers were already bringing back stories of receding glacier fields on K2 mountain in China.

aquifers like a drink through a straw. Aquifers, however, can dry up because of an extended drought or overuse by humans. As the water level, or table, goes down, wells go dry. New ones have to be dug to deeper depths. In some poor parts of the world, such as Africa, people might not have the money or technical resources for this kind of drilling.

Tracking Drought from Space

In Colombo, Sri Lanka, scientists and engineers of different backgrounds tackle issues of drought and water management for the International Water Management Institute (IWMI).

The researchers study conditions on farms and in cities, primarily in Asia and Africa, and offer advice for conserving water where it is scarce.

In recent years, Prasad Thenkabail has been part of IWMI teams examining drought trends in India, Pakistan, and Afghanistan. Governments in the region, particularly Afghanistan's, lack their own research tools for predicting when droughts might occur and how extensive they might be. Dr. Thenkabail and his associates work with the data collected by sensors attached to satellites. The sensors record data such as land surface

∧ A boy helps his family water their land in the Anhui Province of China in 2004. Water shortages have worsened throughout the country since then, resulting in China's current water crisis.

∧ Droughts in Kentucky in 1999 completely dried up a pond in the front of this barn that had been full for the last 80 years.

temperature and the amount of vegetation in a particular region. By comparing past data with current results, the IWMI researchers can pinpoint areas facing a drought.

The Human Factor

Droughts and less severe water shortages can be natural events. But in the future, humans may play a larger part in where they occur and how severe they are. Charlotte de Fraiture, also of IWMI, has focused some of her research on the impact of "green energy" on water use. To reduce the creation of greenhouse gases, nations and companies are looking for new sources of energy. Some people believe that energy should come from biomass—plants such as corn and sugarcane that can be turned into fuel.

China and India are two countries that want to produce more crop-based fuel. But both countries already struggle to meet their water needs. De Fraiture and her team have collected data about water

A Day for Water

In 1992, the United Nations (UN) recognized the growing need to protect water resources and make sure everyone has access to drinking water. Since 1993, every March 22 has been World Water Day. Past years have addressed such topics as water scarcity, ways people celebrate the importance of water, and water-related disasters. In 2008, the focus of the day was sanitation practices to keep water clean to prevent the spread of disease.

The UN also sponsors ongoing scientific research on water through the United Nations Educational, Scientific and Cultural Organization (UNESCO). Two areas of concern are the movement of sea water into coastal aquifers, where it pollutes drinking water, and the need for governments to manage water use. The United Nations also recently backed a historic race to draw attention to the world's water problems. In the Running the Sahara Desert event, three marathoners crossed Africa's Sahara Desert in 111 days, running up to 50 miles (80 km) a day in the extreme heat. Their efforts helped raise $4.5 million for H_2O Africa, an organization devoted to creating awareness of Africa's water crisis and providing clean water in critical areas of the continent.

∧ In 2006, climate change caused the ice of China's No. 1 glacier in the Tianshan Mountains to recede, revealing a previously unknown ice cave.

use and crop production. By using information from the past, they can predict what might happen with water use in the future. Using known information to make predictions is sometimes called modeling. De Fraiture knows how much corn and sugarcane China and India want to use to meet growing energy needs. Her model, called WATERSIM, shows her how much water would be needed to grow those crops. The results tell De Fraiture that the two countries will face severe water shortages if they grow the planned amounts of corn and sugarcane.

Drought or New Desert?

To study changes in the climate and their impact, some scientists rely on powerful computers to process information. One of them is Richard Seager of Columbia University. In 2007, he was the lead author of a report published by the journal *Science*. Seager and his team of scientists analyzed almost 20 different computer models of future trends in temperature and rainfall. Their conclusion: rising temperatures, created by the release of greenhouse gases, will bring droughts to subtropical regions of the world. These are areas just north and south of the tropics, with warm, but not hot, winters. For the United States, the findings mean that the already-dry Southwest, such as Arizona and New

∧ Investigators study the ground of a dried-up reservoir in China's Henan province in June, 2007. The region is the site of the country's most serious drought in 40 years.

Mexico, could experience severe water shortages in the years to come. By as early as 2050, the researchers say, that region could receive 10 to 20 percent less precipitation than it does today. Seager said, "You can't call it a drought anymore, because it's going over to a drier climate. No one says the Sahara is in drought."

< Dr. Richard Seager displaying illustrations of future trends in rainfall, based on his models, on his laptop computer.

Supply and Demand

CHAPTER 4

Waning Resources

Stretching out across Asia, China is the nation with the world's largest population. Some 1.3 billion people live there, and the number rises by 15 million or so each year. In the last 30 years, China has seen remarkable changes. Its economy has boomed as new industries have sprung up across the country. Millions of people who once worked on farms have flocked to cities to take jobs. On the farms, people work hard to grow wheat and other crops to feed the growing population.

Scientists are warning that there is a dark side to China's boom times. The country faces a growing water crisis. Pollution from factories makes some water undrinkable. A 2006 study showed that

< The Nanpu Bridge in Shanghai connects the city to the newly developed region of Pudong. Increased development and industry in the area is affecting the water supply.

∧ A pond in China's Hubei province is separated from the polluted river nearby that feeds it, but residents still must boil water they collect in order to drink it.

almost 30 percent of the water in the Yangtze, China's largest river, was unfit to drink.

The water problems are particularly severe in the North. Farming practices, new industries, and a rapidly increasing population are draining the region's aquifers at a startling rate. Groundwater satisfies about 60 percent of the North China Plain's water needs. But aquifers under the region's main city, Shiajiazhuang, are falling about 4 feet (1.2 m) every year.

The increasing human demand for water is only part of the problem. Precipitation in the region has decreased in recent years, and some scientists say climate change plays a part. Chunmiao Zheng is a hydrologist who works in both China and the United States. He said that climate change has decreased rainfall, so aquifers are not being "recharged,"

and increasing pollution has led to greater contamination of groundwater.

Irrigation Drains Groundwater

Eloise Kendy, a scientist at The Nature Conservancy, has interviewed residents and government officials in the North China Plain about water usage. She combined that information with historical data going back 50 years to model the rate of aquifer recharge in the region. She and the other scientists realized that crop irrigation was the main reason for the groundwater shortage. More land is now irrigated than was irrigated decades ago, and water lost from plants and evaporation from the ground has led to the loss of large amounts of water. One solution for the region may be to build more towns and plant less wheat. Adding more people to the area might seem odd, since in other parts of the world the growth of cities has caused water shortages. But here, water usage would actually be reduced by cutting down on the water loss related to farming.

Water Wars

Around the world, as demand for water rises and supplies fall, many experts see the potential for conflict. Struggles over water are not new. In the early 1900s, the city of Los Angeles purchased land and water rights and began piping in water from rural areas. As the years went on and ranchers in those areas began having difficulties raising crops, some wondered if it was in their best interests to send their water elsewhere, even for a profit.

In recent years, some people have wondered if "water wars" could break out. Chuck Wald, a retired U.S. Air Force general, sees a threat. In 2007, he told Congress that violence in Darfur, Sudan, was partially tied to long periods of drought and the loss of grazing lands. As herders searched for new grazing lands, they entered regions where farmers lived. The two groups then battled each other for the land.

In most cases, two countries sharing water resources are able to cooperate rather than fight. But legal battles over water rights are already happening. In the United States, some people in the western states have eyed the fresh water

Water Consumption in Different World Regions
(in cubic miles)

Area	1995	2000	2010 (projected)	2025 (projected)
Asia	332.3	349.8	382.2	450.1
South America	89	96	106	120
North America	56.9	58.3	61.2	64.5
Europe	45.3	47.2	56.1	61.4
Africa	38.4	40.8	45.8	52.8
Australia and Oceania	4.3	4.6	4.8	5.3

Source: UNESCO

Consumption figures are affected by land area, population, natural distribution of water, and other factors.

∧ Displaced children of war-torn Darfur, Sudan, carry jugs of drinking water provided by international aid agencies.

available in the Great Lakes. The states bordering the lakes, however, are trying to pass laws that would keep the water where it is.

Neighboring states can also battle over access to water. In 2007, Georgia faced a terrible drought. Parts of neighboring Alabama were also touched by the extremely dry weather. Georgia governor Sonny Perdue wanted permission from the U.S. government to reduce the flow out of one of the state's reservoirs. Alabama protested, however, since some of that

water eventually supplies its citizens. Winter rains eased the Georgia drought a bit, but the problem is sure to recur in future years.

In Georgia, some politicians and environmentalists said that perhaps the water problems there could have been avoided. Fewer houses and businesses could have been built in areas where water was in short supply, and more reservoirs could have been dug. Other scientists believe that the reservoirs actually contribute to water shortages by allowing huge quantities of water to evaporate from their surfaces. These same scientists believe that the best way to avoid "water wars" is to improve the way people manage water in its natural settings.

The Search for Safer Water

Even when water is available, it is not always clean. Keeping pollution and human and animal waste out of drinking water is a major problem. More than a billion people in developing nations do not have safe water to drink. The lack of sanitation and good hygiene means that people risk getting cholera or other diseases from drinking unclean water. The problem is huge: Diseases associated with unclean water kill one child every eight seconds somewhere in the world.

Scientists and engineers around the globe are trying to find ways to provide safe, affordable water and sanitation. Part of the answer might

Water Wonders

The search for clean drinking water has led to some creative inventions. In Africa, kids can do their part to provide water for their families when they go out to play. A few spins on the PlayPump® water system, a small, kid-powered merry-go-round, brings up drinking water from aquifers as deep as 300 feet (91 m). As the children spin, they pump up water that goes into a large storage tank aboveground. The water then flows into a tap on the ground that anyone can operate.

∧ **African children play on the PlayPump, a device that pumps groundwater from deep inside the earth to a storage tank above ground.**

Making dirty water safe to drink is the goal of a gadget called the LifeStraw Personal. People use the LifeStraw to drink water just as they would use a regular straw. The inside of the straw is treated with a chemical that kills the organisms that can cause diarrhea. A filter also screens out tiny particles in the water. One LifeStraw provides at least two liters of clean water every day for one year.

lie in experiments with latrines, small stand-alone toilets that can be placed anywhere. Christine Moe is one of the directors of the Center for Global Safe Water at Emory University. She has spent years studying how to improve sanitation in rural areas. In El Salvador, Moe and other researchers studied the waste produced in a variety of latrines. They concluded that solar latrines did the best job of killing the

> **LifeStraw and similar technologies hope to enable millions of people without access to safe drinking water to purify their water wherever they live.**

tiny organisms found in the water. Those organisms, when they enter the water supply, are the source of many deadly diseases in humans.

In 2006, armed with the knowledge that solar power makes for better latrines, some students at Georgia Institute of Technology designed a better version. The trick was to create enough heat to kill the organisms—about 150°F (66°C)—while keeping the inside of the latrine cool for users. The waste was turned into fertilizer. The new model was a success in tests in Bolivia.

Salt Solutions

As noted in Chapter 1, most of the world's water is in the oceans. Because of its salt, ocean water is not fit for drinking. But around the world, desalination plants turn salty water into safe water. Israel recently completed the largest desalination plant in the world. Water from the Mediterranean Sea goes through a set of filters that remove any large particles in it. Then the water passes through a membrane under high pressure that removes the salt in the water. The plant produces about 5 percent of Israel's total water needs.

Australian scientist Ric Pashley also thinks seawater holds the key for plentiful drinking water. In 2005, Pashley released results from work he did with electrodialysis. In this method of desalination, an electrical current is passed through water. The electricity separates sodium

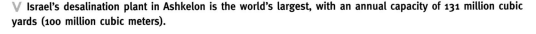

▽ Israel's desalination plant in Ashkelon is the world's largest, with an annual capacity of 131 million cubic yards (100 million cubic meters).

and chloride, the ingredients of salt, from the water, leaving it drinkable. Pashley learned that taking the gases oxygen and nitrogen out of the seawater made it conduct electricity better. When the gases are removed first, electrodialysis is even faster and cheaper.

Two years later, Dr. Pashley reported that he had found still another way to desalinate seawater. It combines two existing methods of desalination: distillation, which involves boiling the water, and the membrane process described in Chapter 1, which is used in Israel and elsewhere. With his method, Pashley heats—but does not boil— the water, and then passes it through membranes that filter out the salt and other unwanted particles. Pashley hopes to build desalination plants that use his new method.

∧ An employee at a desalination plant in El Segundo, California, retrieves a sample of filtrated seawater.

Up on the Roof

Scientists are looking for new ways to meet the thirst for water by increasing the supply. Trees and other plants absorb CO_2, which makes them a key ally in the fight against global warming. But as towns and cities grow, trees and other plants are cut down. One way to get more greenery back into urban areas is with rooftop gardens.

Wayne Mackey, a scientist at Texas A&M University, wants to make it easier and cheaper to build these gardens. He is studying a foam that was developed to keep fuel from moving around inside airplane fuel tanks. The foam also can be used as "soil" for plants. It holds in the air and water that plants need to grow. Having more rooftop gardens would also be good for the water system. "Green" roofs use more of the rainwater for the plants, reducing runoff.

Other opportunities to use water more efficiently include low-flow toilets, drip irrigation lines, and front-loading washing machines. Managing our demand for water is as important as increasing the supply.

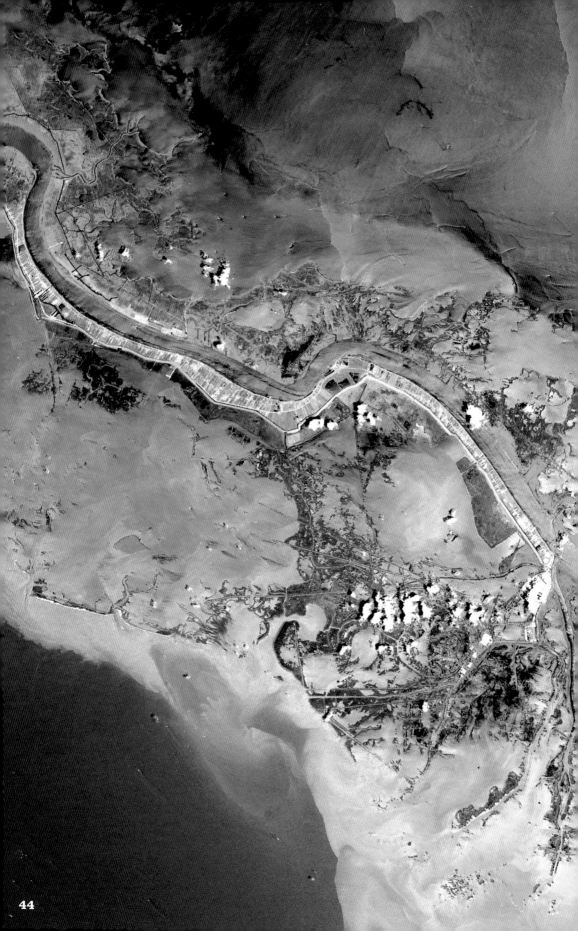

A Continent's Backbone

CHAPTER 5

A Major Source of Water

It starts with a small flow of water, just three feet (0.9144 m) deep, at Minnesota's Lake Itasca. From that point, the mighty Mississippi River rolls on for 2,350 miles (3,781 km), reaching a depth of more than 200 feet (61 m) near New Orleans. At La Crosse, Wisconsin, it spans a width of more than 4 miles (6.4 km). As the Mississippi cuts across the United States on its way to the Gulf of Mexico, waters from other large rivers, including the Missouri and the Ohio, flow into it. All the land over which smaller streams and rivers flow to enter into a larger one is called a watershed or basin. The Mississippi River Basin is the largest in the United States. Including its tributaries, the

< Losing energy as it reaches the Gulf of Mexico, the Mississippi River unloads the sediment it has carried on its journey through the middle of North America, creating the marshlands and mud flats that form the fertile land of the Mississippi River Delta.

river drains water from more than 1.2 million square miles (3.1 million sq km) of land—about 41 percent of the continental United States.

A Joint Effort

Along with the nearby Great Lakes and the Gulf of Mexico, the Mississippi River Basin is part of what has been called the backbone of North America. These waters teem with fish and shellfish that people eat. The Great Lakes and many rivers provide drinking water. The watery backbone is a transportation route for ships that carry goods and passengers. And the Mississippi, Gulf, and Great Lakes provide recreation for boaters,

∧ Researcher Tatsuaki Nakato holds up pearly mussels, one of many species of marine life found in the Mississippi River.

fishers, and swimmers. Ensuring the health of these waters is a major concern of scientists from a variety of fields.

Bringing together many experts in one location is the goal of the Mississippi Riverside Environmental Research Station. Located near Muscatine, Iowa, the research center welcomes geologists, biologists, engineers, and others. The station was the idea of Tatsuaki Nakato, a research engineer at the University of Iowa. "The Mississippi River affects all of us," he said. "As long as humans exist we will need to study it."

At the station, researchers collect samples of water and study them in a lab. They want to see what chemicals are in the water and how they affect the fish that swim in it. The scientists can also track

< Much of U.S. commerce relies on cargo shipments that are carried through the Great Lakes. As the water recedes due to climate change, businesses may be at risk.

changes in the amount of chemicals and gases in the water, to see if conditions improve or worsen over time. Another key issue, according to Nakato, is the amount of soil eroding into the river from its banks. The erosion can affect the quality of drinking water taken from the river.

Great Lakes, Huge Stakes

Not too far east of Lake Itasca, the Mississippi's source, is Lake Superior. It is the westernmost and largest of the five Great Lakes. Some 40 million residents of the United States and Canada count on the Great Lakes for their drinking water.

Keeping tabs on such a vast area of water takes a lot of effort. Scientists rely on satellite images, such as those provided by CoastWatch, part of NOAA. CoastWatch satellites record data such as water temperature and the amount of water vapor in the air. CoastWatch also keeps data collected on the ground, such as wind and current speeds. Using information from CoastWatch, scientists can track ice cover on the lakes or the spread of algae.

Some scientists do their own research along the lakes. Deborah Swackhamer directs the Institute on the Environment at the University of Minnesota. An environmental chemist, Swackhamer has measured pollutants in Lake Superior. Compared with levels in the other four Great Lakes, pollution levels in Lake Superior are low. A growing concern, Swackhamer said, is more development along the lakeshore, because homes and businesses can release new chemicals into the water.

The Great Lakes

	Superior	Michigan	Huron	Erie	Ontario
Elevation (feet)	600	577	577	569	243
Length (miles)	350	307	206	241	193
Breadth (miles)	160	118	183	57	53
Average depth (feet)	483	279	195	62	283
Maximum depth (feet)	1,332	925	750	210	802
Volume (cubic miles)	2,900	1,180	850	116	393
Shoreline (miles)	2,726	1,638	3,827	871	712

Source: NOAA

New Water Worries

Scientists have recently recorded other changes in the Great Lakes. Water temperatures in Lake Superior have risen 4.5°F (2.5°C) since 1979, more than 50 percent higher than the increase in the air temperature. Jay Austin, an oceanographer at the University of Minnesota, has studied historical temperature records for Lake Superior. He said the rates of temperature increase "just go bananas from 1980 to the present... it's, as far as I know, one of the largest changes in temperature of any natural system that's been observed over the last 25 years." Rising temperatures could pose a threat to some fish that live in the lake.

While temperatures have gone up, water levels have fallen in Superior and the other Great Lakes. From about 1997 to 2007, the water level in Lake Superior fell 2 feet (0.6 m). Falling water levels affect shipping because ships have to carry lighter loads to avoid the risk of running aground.

Climate changes play a part in the falling water levels. Melting winter snow brings new water to the lakes. But in recent years, as temperatures have risen, less snow has fallen in the region. Winter ice on the lakes has also decreased. The warmer temperatures and lack of ice cause more water to evaporate from the lakes.

"Strangling" Water

Human activity plays a part in another problem threatening the North American water backbone. The farmland along the Mississippi River and its tributaries is some of the most productive in the world. But to grow their crops, farmers feed the soil with nitrogen and other nutrients. Rain then carries some of these chemicals into the rivers. Industrial chemicals and wastewater also enter the Mississippi system through this runoff. The chemicals flow downstream and eventually reach the Gulf of Mexico. There,

◁ Green algae, also known as "dead man's fingers," sucks the oxygen from the water when it decomposes, creating dead zones for other sea life.

⋀ In 2007, Lake Superior, the coldest and deepest of the Great Lakes, ebbed to its lowest point in nearly 100 years.

they collect and promote the growth of algae, creating what are called blooms. When the algae die and decay, their decomposition takes oxygen out of the water faster than it can be replaced. The lower levels of oxygen mean that other life forms in the Gulf are starved for this essential gas. This condition, similar to strangulation, is called hypoxia. It creates areas where sea life has difficulty surviving. These regions are called dead zones, and the one in the Gulf covers about 8,000 square miles (20,720 sq km). Over time, dead zones threaten the livelihoods of fishers who catch the fish and shellfish in the Gulf.

In 2007, water chemist Wayne Gardner of the University of Texas received funding for a three-year study of the Gulf of Mexico's dead zone. He and his team want to learn what level of nitrogen and oxygen in the water produces the dead zone. With this information, they can create computer models. Gardner said, "Those models are...critical to guiding management of how those nutrients will have to be reduced to get the dead zone down to a reasonable level."

More to Explore

CHAPTER 6

ABE and Brothers

Half a mile below the surface of the Pacific Ocean, a small underwater vehicle is at work. The Autonomous Benthic Explorer (ABE) is mapping the ocean floor. ABE is a robot, about 6 feet (1.8 m) long and weighing 1,200 pounds (544 kg). Scientists program ABE's onboard computer so the robot will travel along a set path underwater. ABE's video camera records images, while sensors measure data such as temperature and magnetic fields.

On this mission sponsored by NOAA, ABE's goal is to provide information about a large underwater volcano called Brothers. Brothers volcano is located in the southwestern Pacific,

< An image of Brothers volcano. A color scale illustrates different areas of depth on the volcano. Depths in the image range from .7 miles (1,200 meters) at the top of the cone (light pink) to 1.2 miles (1,875 meters) (deep purple) at the bottom.

north of New Zealand. Magma—hot liquid rock found within the Earth's interior—rises up beneath Brothers volcano. The magma heats up cold seawater, which then chemically reacts with the rocks within the summit crater of Brothers volcano. Vents form where these reactions take place, acting as mini-geysers that shoot dissolved minerals out into the ocean. Since the first vents were discovered in 1977, the clouds of dark mineral particles have led some scientists to call the hot vents "black smokers." The underwater geysers also send out chemicals that support life unlike any other on the planet. Most life forms require energy from the sun to survive, but the vent dwellers are too deep to receive that energy. Only the chemicals from the vents provide the energy to keep them alive.

Robert W. Embley and Edward T. Baker, two oceanographers on this expedition with ABE, are focusing on producing the most detailed maps ever of Brothers and the surrounding floor. They and the other scientists aboard the research vessel *Sonne*

▽ Robert W. Embley and Edward T. Baker, two oceanographers on this expedition with ABE, are focusing on producing the most detailed maps ever of Brothers and the surrounding seafloor.

are also interested in underwater volcanic activity. Eruptions release huge quantities of gases, including carbon dioxide (CO_2), into the ocean. With ABE's help, Baker and his team can make the first measurements of the amount of CO_2 released. They hope to learn how this CO_2 affects ocean acidity.

Earth's Last Undiscovered Region

The Brothers expedition is an example of the wide variety of research going on now, in and under Earth's oceans. Some of it is designed to address a specific issue, like the amount of CO_2 produced by volcanoes. Some of it simply helps humans get a full picture of the oceans that surround them. More than a century ago, explorers trudged across Antarctica for the first time. The challenge of adding to world knowledge by going where humans had not gone before excited them. Today's—and tomorrow's—scientific explorers get the same kind of thrill when they discover something new and add to our understanding of the oceans. Despite all the work done in recent years, more than 95 percent of the planet's underwater regions are still an unknown world.

What can research in the ocean depths reveal? Perhaps medicines that can fight cancer. Nereus Pharmaceuticals, a drug company in San Diego, was co-founded by William Fenical, an oceanographer at

New AUV on the Block

∧ The new Sentry autonomous underwater vehicle meets the submersible Alvin during a testing expedition off Bermuda in April 2006.

ABE has served scientists well since its first underwater mission in 1996. But in 2008, the Woods Hole Oceanographic Institution launched an improved AUV (autonomous underwater vehicle) called Sentry. Faster than its older "brother," Sentry can also travel deeper and stay underwater longer. Woods Hole researchers are already planning for the next wave of AUVs to come after Sentry. One idea calls for a vehicle that is both an AUV and a ROV. For scanning large areas of the ocean floor, this proposed research craft would travel on its own, as ABE and Sentry do. But to conduct more detailed research in a small area, the new vehicle would be controlled from a surface ship. Plans call for this combined AUV/ROV to reach depths of more than 33,000 feet (10,058 m), about double the distance of existing underwater research vehicles.

the Scripps Oceanographic Institute. The company searches for microbes, tiny life forms that may contain chemicals that can heal. Tests have been done on one medicine made from an organism called Salinispora that lives in sediment on the ocean floor. Nereus's scientists hope the drug will fight several forms of cancer.

The oceans also hold vast amounts of minerals, especially near vents, or black smokers. Getting the minerals out of the water is expensive. Still, as mining costs on the ground rise and as resources disappear, many people believe that the oceans will become a source of minerals. One such person is Steven Scott, a geologist at the University of Toronto. He is associated with a company trying to mine gold, copper, and other minerals in the Pacific Ocean. Scott said that one day, "deep-sea versions of robotic coal-mining machines" will take the minerals from the ocean floor and transport them to ships on the surface. Scott noted that taking oil and natural gas from the ocean depths has been going on for decades.

Preserving a Food Supply

The oceans will continue to be a source of food. Some fish are raised in confined areas and harvested, just as crops are on land. Others are caught in the wild. Sea Grant is a division of NOAA that works with coastal communities on economic development and responsible building practices. Sea Grant scientists are concerned with protecting fisheries in the Great Lakes and elsewhere. They work to increase the amount of fish harvested while trying to preserve the number of fish in the wild.

The Underwater Workhorses

Scientists explore the ocean depths with the help of some advanced machinery. Outside of a submarine or other underwater vessel, humans cannot survive the force of water pressure on their bodies far below the surface. The pressure increases at extreme depths. Deep-water exploration became easier during the 1960s with the creation of a special research vessel named Alvin. Its thick metal hull could protect its two or three occupants at depths of more than 14,000 feet (4,267 m).

Plunging even deeper are remotely operated vehicles such as Jason. A ROV is connected by wires to a surface ship, and crew members aboard the surface ship control its operations. Jason, launched in 1988, can explore 6

Λ The Hercules ROV is equipped with special features which allow it to perform complex scientific tasks while descending to depths of 2.5 miles (4,000 meters).

∧ The submersible known as Alvin is hoisted up onto the deck of the research vessel *Atlantis* in the Gulf of Alaska.

miles (9.7 km) below the ocean's surface. Another popular ROV is Hercules, which is often used by the Institute for Exploration Research.

ABE and other autonomous underwater vehicles are the next advancement over ROVs. They operate independently, with no ties to a surface ship and no one controlling their actions. AUVs are useful when surface conditions, such as ice or rough seas, keep ships from launching and precisely controlling ROVs. An AUV's computer can direct it to cover an area of several thousand feet while traveling over underwater mountains or down into trenches.

Exploring the seas also helps humans understand their past. Ancient ships that sank and old cities that are now underwater hold clues about how humans lived thousands of years ago. One of the experts in this archaeological exploration is Robert Ballard. He is best known for finding the *Titanic,* the supposedly unsinkable ship that hit an iceberg and sank in the North Atlantic in 1912.

Ballard heads the Institute for Exploration Research. On his missions he has explored shipwrecks in the Black Sea and the Great Lakes. Ballard and his team have also explored an area of hot vents called the Lost City. Ballard said, "If the Lost City had been discovered on land instead of 2,100 feet (640 m) under the ocean, it would be a national park as beautiful and compelling as Yellowstone."

Meet a Volcanologist

Dr. Bill Chadwick is an underwater volcanologist with the National Oceanic and Atmospheric Administration vents program and an associate professor at Oregon State University. Dr. Chadwick explores and researches active submarine volcanoes.

◘ What attracted you to underwater volcanic research?

◙ When Mount St. Helens erupted in 1980, I was a geology major in college, and it was eye-opening to me that there were active volcanoes on the U.S. west coast. After college I went to graduate school to learn more. At about the same time, hydrothermal vents were first being discovered. Since most of Earth's volcanism is actually underwater, it seemed natural to blend the two (volcanology and marine science). I think what I like most about it is that it's a scientific frontier. I love the feeling of discovery.

◘ Are underwater eruptions different from eruptions on land?

◙ Yes, definitely. There are two important factors that affect the character of eruptions underwater: pressure and temperature. In underwater eruptions, seawater can cool lava much more quickly than air, and so it sometimes creates a flow called "pillow lava," that only forms underwater.

◘ What is the relationship between underwater volcanoes and hydrothermal vents?

◙ Underwater volcanoes provide the heat source that drives the hydrothermal vents. Cold seawater seeps down into the ocean crust, gets heated up by magma underground, and rises back up to come out at the seafloor. [The hot seawater] basically dissolves the rock it circulates through.

◘ During your 2005 expedition off New Zealand, what kind of biological and chemical samples did you collect near the vents?

◙ We took samples of hydrothermal vent fluids and gases, hydrothermal sediments, and the animals and microbes living at the vents. Whenever we go to new hydrothermal environments, we almost always find new biological species.

🔲 **What is the significance of underwater volcanic eruptions as they relate to increased levels of CO2?**

🔲 Volcanoes do emit CO2, but at levels that are much lower than the amounts humans are putting into the atmosphere from the burning of fossil fuels.

🔲 **What impact do global warming and other changes to the ocean have on your areas of research?**

🔲 A very big area of concern is ocean acidification. A large part of the CO2 we put into the atmosphere is absorbed by the ocean, and the increased CO2 makes seawater more acidic. It will be harder for animals that make shells to live (including coral reefs, shellfish, and even some plankton). We are using some underwater volcanic sites with high CO2 and biological communities as natural laboratories to study the potential impacts of ocean acidification.

🔲 **What is it like traveling in Pisces (and other submersibles) to such deep underwater regions?**

🔲 I've made dives in Pisces and Alvin. I remember my first dive very clearly. On your way down to the bottom, you see bioluminescent creatures

∧ **Dr. Bill Chadwick (left) studies data in the control room of the ROV Jason during a dive. Video screens display images of the sea floor.**

drifting by the windows of the sub—it's very magical. Then once we got to the bottom it was really mind-blowing to look out the window and see the BOTTOM OF THE OCEAN! Nowadays, I mostly use remotely operated vehicles.

🔲 **What are some of the benefits of studying the vents and the life-forms near them? Will there be practical results that people can use?**

🔲 Life on Earth may have started at deep-sea hydrothermal vents (some of the most primitive microbes are found there), so in a way we're exploring our own beginnings. Exploring the extreme environments where life can exist on Earth tells us under what conditions life might be possible on other planets. Some of the more practical benefits are in biotechnology, where enzymes found in heat-loving microbes from seafloor hot springs are used to perform rapid chemical reactions to copy DNA in laboratories

around the world.

🔲 **What is your next scientific expedition?**

🔲 My next expedition will be in about a year (spring 2009) to a submarine volcano called NW Rota-1 in the Mariana volcanic arc (north of Guam). We witnessed underwater explosive eruptions at this volcano for the first time from 2004 to 2006. It is an extraordinary place because the pressure at 550 meters depth (where the eruptive vent is) subdues the eruptions enough that they can be observed at close range (with an ROV). I think we learn the most about these kinds of processes by watching them in action.

🔲 **What should we all know about the importance of the oceans and the dangers they face?**

🔲 Our lives depend on the oceans. We should treat them that way.

What Lies Ahead

Λ Scientist Andy Billings of the Woods Hole Oceanographic Institution checks on ABE before its dive at Brothers volcano.

Research at the sanctuaries is just one part of the never-ending effort to understand the water that surrounds us. As you've learned, the world faces a variety of problems connected to water, with a growing shortage of drinkable water at the top of the list. From glaciers high in the mountains, to rivers, to water deep below the ground, people get water from many sources. Unfortunately, human activity creates some of the issues that make it hard to ensure we always have enough clean water for everyone—and for the plants and animals that rely on it as well.

Creating solutions for the world's water needs may also be about keeping peace around the world.

It will become necessary to blur our borders and work together to combat the effects of climate change so that people in every nation can be assured health and prosperity in the future. There is great hope for solving our water problems, whether by tapping the oceans for drinking water or changing our actions that threaten water supplies. Research, in the field and in the lab, will play a part in solving those problems— and expanding our knowledge about this precious resource.

Glossary

algae — plant-like life form usually found in water

benthic — relating to or occurring at the bottom of a body of water

contamination — the addition of a harmful substance

crust — the hard outer layer of Earth

evaporate — to change into a vapor

expedition — a trip taken to explore

fossils — the remains of ancient life forms, such as bones or footprints that harden in rocks

glacier — a large body of ice that moves slowly across land

hydrologist — a scientist who studies the properties and circulation of water in all its forms

hygiene — sanitary conditions and actions that promote health

irrigation — taking water from streams or other sources to grow crops

membrane — a thin skin or piece of material that lets some liquids or solids pass through but not others

molecules — the smallest bits of a substance that have all the properties of that substance

nutrients — chemicals needed for life forms to survive and grow

tributary — a source of water, such as a stream or small river, that flows into a larger river

tropics — area of Earth immediately north and south of the Equator, marked by warm temperatures year-round

vapor — a substance in the form of a gas

< Andean glaciers (seen in background) have lost 22 percent of their area since 1970. According to scientists at Peru's National Resources Institute, the meltdown has sped up in recent years.

Bibliography

Books

Kandel, Robert. *Water from Heaven: The Story of Water from the Big Bang to the Rise of Civilization and Beyond.* New York: Columbia University Press, 2003.

Stow, Dorrik. *Oceans: An Illustrated Reference.* Chicago: University of Chicago Press, 2006.

Articles

Kunzig, Robert. "Drying of the West." NATIONAL GEOGRAPHIC (February 2008): 90–108.

Further Reading

Barr, Gary. *Climate Change: Is the World in Danger?* Chicago: Heinemann Library, 2007.

Earle, Sylvia. *Dive! My Adventures in the Deep Frontier.* Washington, D.C.: National Geographic Society, 1998.

Kramer, Nash. *Water.* Washington, D.C.: National Geographic Society, 2005.

McMillan, Beverly. *Oceans.* New York: Simon & Schuster Books for Young Readers, 2007.

Miller, Debra A., ed. *Will the World Run Out of Fresh Water?* Detroit: Greenhaven Press, 2007.

Shoveller, Herb. *Ryan and Jimmy and the Well in Africa That Brought Them Together.* Tonawanda, NY: Kids Can Press, 2006.

Smuskiewicz, Alfred J. *Properties of Water.* Milwaukee: Gareth Stevens, 2007.

On the Web

Blue Frontier: Oceans for Life
http://www.nationalgeographic.com/features/seas/

International Polar Year
http://www.ipy.org/index.php

NOAA—National Sea Grant Office
http://www.seagrant.noaa.gov/

NOAA—Ocean Explorer
http://oceanexplorer.noaa.gov/

Oceans Alive
http://www.oceansalive.org/home.cfm

Scripps Institution of Oceanography
http://sio.ucsd.edu/

Water Science for Schools: The Water Cycle
http://ga.water.usgs.gov/edu/watercycle.html

Woods Hole Oceanographic Insitution
http://www.whoi.edu/

⋀ A previously buried section of the Great Wall of China emerged as the Panjiakou Reservoir in China's Hebel province dried up in July 2000.

Index

Boldface indicates illustrations.

∧ The research vessel *Roger Revelle* encountered an iceberg floating in the Indian Ocean in February 2008. The crew on the ship is studying changes in the chemical makeup of the ocean over the past decade.

About the Author

Michael Burgan has been writing about many different subjects for children and young adults for over 10 years. His work has been published in *The New York Times, Sports Illustrated for Kids*, and *National Geographic World,* among others. A former writer for Weekly Reader Corporation, Michael has developed products for online use and produced educational materials to be used by teachers. He holds a Bachelor of Arts degree in History from the University of Connecticut.

Consultant

Dr. Peter H. Gleick loves water. Trained as an environmental scientist at Yale University and the University of California, Berkeley, Gleick combines science, policy, economics, and culture into a new way of thinking about our water resources— a "soft path" to a sustainable future. He did some of the earliest research into how human-caused climatic changes will affect water resources, why people to fight over water resources and how to reduce those conflicts, and ways to use water efficiently to do what humans want to do, while still protecting natural ecosystems. He is co-founder and President of the non-profit Pacific Institute in Oakland, California (www.pacinst.org) and was elected to the U.S. National Academy of Sciences. He is also the recipient of the prestigious MacArthur Foundation "genius" award. His greatest achievement was two fine boys—a joint production with his wife, Nicki Norman, a science educator.

Founded in 1888, the National Geographic Society is one of the largest nonprofit scientific and educational organizations in the world. It reaches more than 285 million people worldwide each month through its official journal, *National Geographic,* and its four other magazines; the National Geographic Channel; television documentaries; radio programs; films; books; videos and DVDs; maps; and interactive media. National Geographic has funded more than 8,000 scientific research projects and supports an education program combating geographic illiteracy.

For more information, please call 1-800-NGS LINE (647-5463) or write to the following address:

National Geographic Society
1145 17th Street N.W., Washington, D.C.
20036-4688 U.S.A.

Visit us online at
www.nationalgeographic.com/books

For librarians and teachers:
www.ngchildrensbooks.com

More for kids from National Geographic:
kids.nationalgeographic.com

For information about special discounts for bulk purchases, please contact National Geographic Books Special Sales: ngspecsales@ngs.org

For rights or permissions inquiries, please contact National Geographic Books Subsidiary Rights: ngbookrights@ngs.org

Library of Congress Cataloging-in-Publication Data available upon request

Hardcover ISBN: 978-1-4263-0360-9
Library ISBN: 978-1-4263-0267-1

Printed in China

Book design by Dan Banks, Project Design Company

Published by the National Geographic Society

John M. Fahey, Jr., *President and Chief Executive Officer;* Gilbert M. Grosvenor, *Chairman of the Board;* Tim T. Kelly, *President, Global Media Group;* John Q. Griffin, *President, Publishing;* Nina D. Hoffman, *Executive Vice President; President, Book Publishing Group*

Prepared by the Book Division

Nancy Laties Feresten, *Vice President, Editor in Chief, Children's Books;*
Bea Jackson, *Director of Design and Illustrations, Children's Books;*
Amy Shields, *Executive Editor, Series, Children's Books*

Staff for This Book

Virginia Ann Koeth, *Editor*
Jim Hiscott, *Art Director*
Lori Epstein, *Illustrations Editor*
Stuart Armstrong, *Graphics*
Lewis R. Bassford, *Production Manager*
Grace Hill, *Associate Managing Editor*
Jennifer A. Thornton, *Managing Editor*
R. Gary Colbert, *Production Director*
Susan Borke, *Legal and Business Affairs*

Manufacturing and Quality Management

Christopher A. Liedel, *Chief Financial Officer*
Phillip L. Schlosser, *Vice President*
Chris Brown, *Technical Director*
Nicole Elliott, *Manager*

Photo Credits

Front: Frans Lemmens/zefa/Corbis
Back & Spine: Mehau Kulyk/Photo Researchers, Inc.
Back Icon: Kmitu/Shutterstock

AP = Associated Press; 1, Associated Press; 2-3, 4 Photoa.com; 6, NautilisMinerals; 8, courtesy Dr. Peter H. Gleick; 10, USGS; 10, Image courtesy of New Zealand American Submarine Ring of Fire 2007 Exploration, NOAA Vents Program, the Institute of Geological & Nuclear Sciences and NOAA-OE, 11, Brenda LeRoux Babin, LUMCON; 11, iStock; 11, Associated Press; Peter Essick/Aurora/Getty Images; 12-13, Peter Essick/Aurora/Getty Images ; 14, Christian Wiencke/Alfred-Wegener-Institut, German; 15 (top), Katharina Zacher/Alfred-Wegener-Institut, German; 15 (bottom), Alfred-Wegener-Institut, German; 16, Scott Doughety/Lawrence Livermore National Laboratory; 17 (top and bottom), iStock; 19, Island Sun photo; 20-21, Rich Reid/National Geographic/Getty Images; 22 (top), Russ Hopcroft; 22 (bottom), NOAA; 23, 24, Photo provided by Richard Feely; 25 (top and bottom), Dr. Richard Norris, Scripps Institution of Oceanography; 26, Library of Congress; 27 (top), NASA, 27 (bottom) Associated Press; 28-29, Courtesy of Tomás Munit; 30, Courtesy of L.G. Thompson, Byrd Polar Research Center, The Ohio State University; 31, Courtesy of Tomás Munita; 31, 32, 33, 34, 35 (top), Associated Press; 35 (bottom), Courtesy of Richard Seager; 36-37, Rafael Macia / Photo Researchers, Inc.; 38, 40, Associated Press; 41 (top), Frimmel Smith; 41 (bottom) Vestergaard Frandsen; 42, Israel Sun/Yael Tzur /Landov ; 43, Associated Press; 44-45, Science Source; 46 (top), Courtesy of Tatsuaki Nakato; 46 (bottom), Associated Press; 48, NOAA, 49, Associated Press; 50-51, 52, Image courtesy of New Zealand American Submarine Ring of Fire 2007 Exploration, NOAA Vents Program, the Institute of Geological & Nuclear Sciences and NOAA-OE; 53, Chris German, Woods Hole Oceanographic Institution; 55 (top), OAR/National Undersea Research Program (NURP); Woods Hole Oceanographic Institution; 55 (bottom), NOAA; 56, Kelly Chadwick; 57, Lance Wills; 58, Image courtesy of New Zealand American Submarine Ring of Fire 2007 Exploration, NOAA Vents Program, the Institute of Geological & Nuclear Sciences and NOAA-OE. 59, 60, Associated Press; 63, Photo taken by Chief Engineer Paul Mauricio

Front cover: Namibian boy drinking water from a tap
Back cover: Empty plastic water bottle

Page 1: A Sudanese woman carries water supplies at the refugee camp of Gallap, west of the Darfur town of Al-Fasher, Sudan, June 14, 2006.

Pages 2–3: The majority of our planet is made up of water, but relatively little of it is fit to use for irrigation or drinking unless it is treated.

A Creative Media Applications, Inc. Production

Editor: Susan Madoff
Copy Editor: Laurie Lieb
Design and Production: Luís Leon and Fabia Wargin